Beyond the Shadows
of Doubt

Copyright © 2024 by Tabatha Rewis

Beyond the Shadows of Doubt:

Imperfect Faith for Perfect Peace

by Tabatha Rewis

Printed in the United States of America.

Cover Design, Edited and Formatted by CSC Professional Editing & Creative Writing Services; Published by CSC Professional Editing & Creative Writing Services

All rights reserved solely by the author. The author guarantees all contents are original and do not infringe upon the legal rights of any other person or work. No part of this book may be reproduced in any form without the permission of the author. The views expressed in this book are not necessarily those of the publisher.

Scriptures marked NLT are taken from the HOLY BIBLE, NEW LIVING TRANSLATION (NLT): Scriptures taken from the HOLY BIBLE, NEW LIVING TRANSLATION, Copyright© 1996, 2004, 2007 by Tyndale House Foundation. Used by permission of Tyndale House Publishers, Inc., Carol Stream, Illinois 60188. All rights reserved. Used by permission.

Scriptures marked ESV are taken from the THE HOLY BIBLE, ENGLISH STANDARD VERSION (ESV): Scriptures taken from THE HOLY BIBLE, ENGLISH STANDARD VERSION ® Copyright© 2001 by Crossway, a publishing ministry of Good News Publishers. Used by permission.

Scriptures marked MSG are taken from the THE MESSAGE: THE BIBLE IN CONTEMPORARY ENGLISH (TM): Scripture taken from THE MESSAGE: THE BIBLE IN CONTEMPORARY ENGLISH, copyright©1993, 1994, 1995, 1996, 2000, 2001, 2002. Used by permission of NavPress Publishing Group

Scripture quotations are from New Revised Standard Version Bible, copyright © 1989 National Council of the Churches of Christ in the United States of America. Used by permission. All rights reserved worldwide.

Beyond the Shadows of Doubt:

Imperfect Faith for Perfect Peace

By Tabatha Rewis

Dedication

For Col, my miracle baby-turned-grown-man, without whom I would never have seen or experienced the depth of love from our Lord that I've been able to witness these past few years with you. I'm always praying - and never letting go. Love you more than you know.

For my husband, Jerry, who has taught me as much in our home as he has in the pulpit. Thank you for being my sounding board, my coach, my mentor and my theologian. Love you for eternity!

And for the readers who may be struggling to live up to the "perfect faith" hype: you're not alone. We're in this fight together, and I can't wait to hear your story of imperfect faith!

Table of Contents

Introduction..................................pg. 9

Chapter 1: Light & Shadows....................pg. 11

Chapter 2: Under the Shadow...................pg. 23

Chapter 3: Faith is a Decision................pg. 31

Chapter 4: Doubt Vs. Decision.................pg. 37

Chapter 5: The "Doubt Is Sin" Debate..........pg. 45

Chapter 6: Worshiping In the Darkness.........pg. 69

Chapter 7: Suit Up in Armor...................pg. 75

Chapter 8: Faith Despite Doubt................pg. 87

Chapter 9: Faith = Trust + Confidence.........pg. 91

Chapter 10: God Loves Doubters................pg. 101

Scripture References..........................pg. 109

About the Author..............................pg. 115

Introduction

I thought I had decently strong faith. My husband and I ministered for years, teaching others how to be faithful. Then we were thrust head first into my son's life decisions, and I wound up questioning and doubting my own decisions as well as my own faith.

This book, the testimony and lessons within are the culmination of many years of my walk with Christ. I'm learning how to walk in the shadows, but not be overtaken by them. I've learned lessons from victories, but also lessons from painful battle scars. Please understand, I'm not completely out of the shadows. Each day is not filled with heavenly clouds and cherubs feeding me grapes. There are still times I have to lean HEAVILY on what I've learned about faith and doubt. But through these lessons, I am able to navigate my doubts and imperfections with a peace that would have seemed impossible just a few years ago. You could say it is a peace that surpasses understanding. It is my imperfect faith coupled with His perfect peace that has enabled me to see glimmers of light even amidst the darkness of doubt.

In life, there's really no such thing as perfect faith! God knows my faith is not perfect, by any means. I've learned it's ok to have doubts along the way; it's our times of doubt that ultimately make our faith in God stronger in the end. Understanding that doubt is a temporary burden that can be let go, rather than a sin that defines our soul forever, has brought me an indescribable sense of freedom. That is why I believe this book needs to be in your hands.

You too can break free from the shadows of doubt. And once you do, you will be amazed at how different those same shadows appear when viewed from outside their grasp.

I know now, Lord, why you utter no answer. You are yourself the answer.

-C.S. Lewis

Chapter 1

Light & Shadows

Journal Entry

11/27/2022

This morning, we gathered as a family and made our way to church. I am grateful for this small moment of togetherness amidst the chaos that has consumed us. But deep down, I feel numb and overwhelmed with emotions. My husband has barely said a handful of words in the last three days, like he's still in some sort of silent shock since our son has shared his news. But we are headed to church as a family to "do" church, I guess.

Yes, I'm glad our son is here with us today instead of being in the mental health facility where we were not allowed to see him for several days. And where we finally were allowed to come pick him up on Thanksgiving Day, the day when everything changed. I am grateful to hear his breathing as we drive to church together, but I can't help but worry about how much longer he will be with us if he follows through with his decisions. He wants to go down a path that goes against everything we have taught him and believed in. How do I reconcile this with the words God spoke to me about his life just a few months ago?

When I was worried about which college he would choose, God told me that He had plans for my son, and I needed to let go of my own plans for him. But how could this be part of God's plan? To have my son turn his back on his faith, his upbringing, and even his own family?

I thought things were getting better, but now it seems like he may have been lying to us or still hiding the truth from us. Or perhaps he wasn't lying and simply fell deeper into a lifestyle he claimed to be leaving behind. Regardless, I am worried about his next steps, which might lead him down a path that cannot be undone or reversed.

I'm worried for my baby. I'm scared. My fear is that he will always be lost after this. It feels like I am racing against time itself to save my son's soul.

My sweet little boy used to quote Bible verses and impressed everyone at Children's Church by singing

"The Lord's Prayer" in its original form. It was adorable and they let him finish the whole song.

He once prayed with such strong faith, even at the young age of four, for God to heal his Poppy of his "drug" addiction - which turned out to be the cigarettes my father smoked since his youth on my grandparents' farm. He used to volunteer tirelessly at church without complaint, even through his teenage years.

This is the same son who fought insecurities and battled depression, but seemed to have found true peace when he testified in front of our congregation seven months ago about feeling God's touch for the first time in his life. This is the miracle baby we prayed for before conception. And when we finally conceived, the overwhelming joy and immense responsibility collided, and we prayed even more earnestly over his life while my body was nurturing his.

But now, it seems like he is turning away from his faith and our spiritual community. I could maybe handle him walking away from this way of life, but what breaks my heart is him turning away from the God he once knew. How could I accept an eternity without my own child if he doesn't turn back to God?

I knew I couldn't face life without a relationship with my son. He would always have a place in our home, our family; wherever God would take us, there would be room for him too. There had to be. He needed to know that even if we didn't agree, he was still a part of us. But I am so scared.

I am pleading with God to remove the blinders of deception from my son's eyes so he can see clearly again. He has been so influenced by society's smoke and mirrors that he can no longer distinguish truth from the lies. As he told me, "That may be your truth, but it's not mine."

God, help my son to SEE, really see, YOUR TRUTH. And give him whatever it is he needs to feel confident in YOUR love, Your sovereignty, Your provision. Help him to see the real love You have for him is better than any "love" he could imagine. Show him the truth of what real love is. Help him to see the distinction of love for friends and humankind and the love he is so desperately seeking.

God, ignite a fire inside of him for Your Word, Your truth, Your spirit and presence, that cannot be extinguished or stifled. You've called him. You've spoken over him. You said YOU had plans for him. Show him those plans and how much better they are than the one he's pursuing. God, cause your plans to overtake every plan and lie of the enemy so that Col can clearly see and feel immense peace with following YOUR plan.

Help me to see Your plans too, especially for how I can help my son.

Reading back over the journal entry from that Thanksgiving weekend still brings a wave of hopelessness, panic, and despair. It was just a few months prior that my son left for college, and as a mama bear, I was already stressed about him being away from home. My son, Col (yes, we're one of those families who spelled their child's name differently), has always been incredibly intelligent, musically gifted, and funny - but I'm not saying that because he's my son. He has a natural charm and is respectful of others, although on the quieter side. However, he never hesitated to lend a helping hand or make someone smile. Throughout his childhood and teenage years, he gave us so many reasons to be proud of him. We even nicknamed him the "Golden Child" at one point because of his sun-kissed appearance and sweet, innocent demeanor.

But please understand, I am not saying he was perfect. I wasn't blinded by love. He just had a way of making things look effortless that others may have found difficult at times. So when he left for college, we were proud of his independence.

At this time, I was working full-time in a job that I loved (and still do) and also enrolled in a program called Calling And Ministries Studies to get my ministerial license. My husband had earned his credentials years ago, but I only recently felt it was the right time for me to pursue them as well. Our church was thriving both numerically and spiritually under our leadership. I was delving deeper into my relationship with God through studying His Word like never before. We were in a good place - busy and occasionally stressful - but overall great.

That Thanksgiving marked what we thought was the longest week of our lives as parents. A week prior, Col called me late at night to tell me that one of his friends had taken him to the ER. Trying not to panic, I asked all the necessary questions while trying to keep both of us calm. He explained that a classmate had been worried about him and took him to the campus counselor, who was concerned about his thoughts of suicide.

Even now, I remember Col downplaying the gravity of the situation. In his mind, he probably thought they would just talk to a doctor and then make an appointment for him to see a therapist. But the ER doctor deemed it serious enough to file a 1013 form - which, in our state, allows for involuntary admission to a mental health facility.

During our call, Col mentioned that they were considering sending him somewhere for psychiatric evaluation, but they needed to find an available bed first. Meanwhile, he was still at the ER. I prayed with him for wisdom and peace, terrified because of the horror stories I had heard about people leaving our local mental health facilities worse than when they went in. And then, like something out of a Hollywood script, Col's phone died mid-conversation.

Throughout the night, I repeatedly tried calling his phone to see if he had been able to charge it. I had heard that during times of mental crises, most facilities would confiscate cell phones until patients were discharged. However, I held onto the hope that they would allow him a call since his parents had no idea where he was - or if he was ok.

The next day, I received a call from an unfamiliar number after not hearing from Col for about 15 hours since his phone died. When I answered, my 18-year-old son's panic-ridden voice came through: "Mom, you have got to come get me! I can't stay here! I'm not supposed to be here but they won't let me leave!" I tried to soothe him as much as I could, my heart breaking knowing that I couldn't get to him. As much as we wanted to, those close to us who knew the situation advised us that since Col was legally an adult and under a 1013 hold, there was nothing we could do until his psychologists deemed him mentally stable enough to be released. He was able to tell me where they'd transferred him; around 6am that morning, they finally found an available bed at a facility an hour away.

I remember telling him to try and make the most of his time there. While he hadn't disclosed how dark his mental state had become, I knew he was struggling. My advice was for him to use this opportunity to focus on his mental health without any distractions. I was able to calm him a bit by helping him to see this could be good, if he'd let it be. He shared with me that he had already started writing in a journal they gave him.

After a few minutes, I could hear the nurse in the background telling Col that his time was up, so we ended the call with Col's promise to call back as soon as he could for more updates.

That week was filled with anxiety for all of us. They moved Col to a different facility with different providers once they learned that he was covered under my insurance. But after his panicked call begging me to come get him, we didn't hear from him for almost 48 hours. And because he was over 18 years old, no facility would confirm or deny if he was a patient there due to HIPAA laws. We had no idea where our son was, or if he was ok. Thank God the counselor at Col's college (who had originally sent Col to the ER) checked in with us and learned that we were nearly at our wits' end not knowing anything about where or how he was. She was able to get word to the facility and pulled whatever strings needed so that they would let Col call us late one night to check in with us.

After doing some research, we assumed Col would only be held for the mandatory 72 hours of his 1013 hold. However, after everything was said and done, the doctors determined that he needed to stay longer. He ended up staying in the facility for a week, during which we were able to speak with him every night after the initial 72 hours had passed.

My husband and I lived in a constant state of hyper-anxiety. Unable to know if our son was REALLY okay, or if it was just the medications they were pumping into him. We were grateful for the five minutes we were able to speak to him each night. We prayed for him constantly. While I was at work, I played worship music in the background of completing my tasks, silent prayers for him rolling over and over in my spirit.

Sometimes it was just, *Jesus, keep my baby safe.* Other times, especially in my car driving to and from work, it was downright warfare for his peace, health, confidence, wisdom, identity and calling.

Finally, we received news that we could pick up our son on Thanksgiving morning at 10am. It was a huge relief for this mama who had been anxiously waiting to wrap her arms around her (grown) baby boy and see with her own eyes that he was indeed okay.

Looking back, I guess it's ironic that everything would come crashing down on the day we set aside to give thanks to God for our family and our blessings. That Thanksgiving would be much, much different. When we arrived at the facility, we had to wait on the guard to unlock the door, before being led into the lobby to sit on uncomfortably sagging, dingy couches while they found Col and got him to sign the rest of his discharge paperwork. After twenty or so minutes, someone escorted my 6'2" son, still in his robe and pajamas, his long hair unbrushed and matted. He carried a paper bag with his few belongings from his time in the hospital.

When I saw him, something felt off, something different, maybe even wrong. But I pushed the thought down, relieved that we were finally in the same room and my son was going home where he belonged that day, and held my taller-than-me boy until he laughingly pushed me away.

We made it to the car, and it was in that car, driving through the streets of that neighboring town we were able to have our first real conversation in weeks. Lots of things came out into the open that day. And to be honest, I wasn't prepared for a single one of them.

Chapter 2

Under the Shadow

  Col gave us an ultimatum that day. Among other things, he believed we had shoved our religion down his throat, and never gave him the opportunity to decide to have faith or not. In his mind, we (Christians) were brainwashed and we were doing the same to our children, indoctrinating them with a myth. He found evidence to support his claims from YouTube personalities who presented one-sided arguments against the validity of the Bible's God, His commandments, and His laws.

  Because of this, having assumed that his Christian, pastoring parents wouldn't want anything to do with a son who didn't believe and act like they did, Col had made up his mind that he would just have to figure out life without his parents. He told us of several changes that would be coming that we of course couldn't agree with, but by not agreeing with him, Col assumed we wouldn't accept him at all.

My husband and I had been in ministry our entire marriage (and years before as well). Loving and serving God had been a part of my life for longer than I'd been with my husband, and when we planned to have a family, we just knew - it was never even a question, really - that our children would be as head-over heels in love with the Lord and His church as we were. And so, Col has been around "church" all his life.

While his daddy and I were serving on the platform or classrooms at church, Col was in the nursery, children's church, or being doted on by church grannies and other kids' parents and grandparents. So in the moment he told us that he wasn't sure if the God we served and professed was the God he wanted to believe in at all, we were crushed. Not because we were disappointed in him, but because after all we did to serve and worship and teach...where did we go wrong that he didn't believe? And the fact that he was so willing to walk away from our family because we believed and he didn't; it was devastating.

Although I struggled to believe it as it was so new, I now believe that we did our best to nurture and raise our son lovingly in the faith and belief in the Lord. But as I tried to find peace amidst the heartbreak, my own faith in the God I had served for years would waver, at times flickering like a candle in a windstorm, desperate to find enough fuel to just keep flickering.

All of us were in uncharted territory. Trying to hold our own family together, trying to show God's love when we felt we were dying inside, trying to keep on keeping on because things still had to get done at church, work and home. That Thanksgiving night, we kept the plans we had made with my mother and sister's family and tried to be as normal as possible. But even my sister's longtime boyfriend told her afterwards, "There's something *bad* wrong with Jerry and Tabby."

There was no denying it, something was wrong. For three days straight, I didn't even hear my husband's voice because he was in such a state of shock over everything that had transpired. He was consumed with thoughts of failing our son and letting down God and the church as the head of our household. And for me, the mom-guilt was overwhelming. What kind of mom was I if my own son couldn't see how real God was to us? Did we not live out our faith enough at home? What could we have done differently? How could our son reject everything he had learned about God after feeling

His touch at a youth conference just a few months before?

As time went on, the "deeper walk" with God that I had grown so comfortable with became more like a cruel and grueling cliffhanger. Despite all my efforts to keep going and serve others, I realized that I was merely going through the motions. On the outside, I had scriptures taped to my mirror and prayed them over my family and son - but deep down, it felt like those prayers were bouncing off an invisible wall. I continued to praise and worship at church, giving it my all during events and gatherings as if everything depended on me.

But when I was alone - on drives to work or sitting in silence while everyone else laughed together - the truth came out. At night, lying next to my sleeping husband while my mind raced, I knew that my faith was running dry. It got to the point where I can only describe it as a spiritual shock. And in those dark moments, my prayers were reduced to two simple words repeated over and over: "Oh Lord... Oh Lord…"

I was studying, worshiping, teaching and praising. But I was also slowly dying. Deep down, I felt like a dying flame, barely flickering at the edge of a dark forest. As days went by, the shadows grew longer and heavier until they enveloped me completely.

My son's doubts and arguments against our faith lingered in the back of my mind, trying to chip away at the foundation of my beliefs. And as they grew louder, other questions emerged from the darkness. How could I continue to preach about trusting in God when I wasn't even sure of my own beliefs? What if everything I thought I knew about God was wrong? What if we lost the battle we were going through? What if all this work for the Lord turned out to be for nothing? What if there was no afterlife and everything we believed was a lie? These thoughts consumed me, making it hard to ignore them any longer.

Yes, this southern, Pentecostal pastor's wife got to the point that I wasn't even sure I believed what my husband and I had been preaching for over 25 years in ministry. And then, of course, almost immediately following all those questions in my mind…would come these questions: How can I be a Christian and have this much doubt? What kind of Christian am I? What kind of leader am I if I'm not CERTAIN in who and what I believe? And I'd scream at myself inwardly, Who do you think you are? You're such a hypocrite!

I know I'm probably not the only one who's dealt with this. You know, then you doubt, and then you feel guilty for doubting. You want to have the faith that you've seen of those faith warriors, those who have had drastic life transformations because of their faith. But right then, when you're in the midst of your own struggles, on the edge between the shadows and what lies beyond, you feel like you don't even know how to FIND that faith. Maybe you, too, have started to think to yourself: What kind of child of God LOSES their faith? Did I really even have it to begin with?

A few months later, I was invited by a dear friend to attend a Christian Women's Retreat in the mountains. It was more than seven hours away from our small town, but because she meant so much to me, I knew I had to go. However, I had no idea what to expect. As someone once joked, multi-denominational worship gatherings are like a box of cereal - you're bound to find some nuts and flakes mixed in there somewhere.

I didn't know what to expect, but I knew I couldn't keep on trying to "fake it 'til I make it". I knew I NEEDED SOMETHING and I was hoping, even though I felt like I didn't have the words to pray anymore, that something would happen.

During the opening session, we were singing and praising together. I worshipped, even though I felt somewhat distant from God. I felt compelled to go up and ask for prayer. It was almost like giving up and just thinking, "Well, might as well try." Although my faith felt lost, I still had a glimmer of hope that something would happen during this weekend. And I was right - it turned out to be so much more than just a girls' weekend.

There were two ladies who prayed with me that night. And I was honest. Brutally honest. I told them that I was a pastor's wife, and that we were facing difficult family issues, and my faith was almost gone. Without hesitation, they prayed for me. It wasn't one of those loud, forceful, jerking and jumping type of prayers that I expected. In fact, we didn't even use anointing oil, as a lot of Pentecostal and Charismatic churches would! It was rather a quiet, sincere and powerful prayer. As these kind women prayed for my faith to be restored, tears streamed down my face as I mourned its loss. But then, in the midst of their prayers, I heard a voice speaking to my soul: **FAITH IS A DECISION.**

Chapter 3:

Faith is a Decision

Faith is a decision? All this time, I thought faith was something we automatically received when we became Christians. I never would have guessed that it was a decision we had to make. What does it even mean?

Tears still streaming down my cheeks, I returned to my seat, bewildered by this new revelation. The idea stuck with me long after the retreat had ended and I was back at home; like Mary, I pondered it in my heart. It wasn't until a few months later that I even told my husband about it. It wasn't just the shock of realizing that everything I thought about faith was wrong; it was also coming to terms with the fact that God Himself noticed my struggles and chose to reveal this nugget of truth to me at just the right time.

For weeks, I couldn't stop thinking about those words: Faith is a decision. And so, I turned to the Author of faith and began diving deeper into what it truly meant. Now, let me clarify one thing: there is also a spiritual gift of faith, as mentioned in 1 Corinthians 12:9 ("to another faith by the same Spirit"). While all believers possess some level of faith, there are some who have been given a special ability to trust God beyond what seems humanly possible. This is not the type of faith we are discussing here. Instead, I am referring to the everyday kind of faith that allows us to KEEP MOVING FORWARD, even when we can only see shadows ahead of us and have no idea what lies beyond them.

As I delved deeper into studying about this type of faith, I was drawn to a familiar story that many of us know well.

"One of the men in the crowd spoke up and said, 'Teacher, I brought my son so you could heal him. He is possessed by an evil spirit that won't let him talk. And whenever this spirit seizes him, it throws him violently to the ground. Then he foams at the mouth and grinds his teeth and becomes rigid. So I asked your disciples to cast out the evil spirit, but they couldn't do it.'

"Jesus said to them, 'You faithless people! How long must I be with you? How long must I put up with you? Bring the boy to me.' So they brought the boy. But when the evil spirit saw Jesus, it threw the child into a violent convulsion, and he fell to the ground, writhing and foaming at the mouth. 'How long has this been happening?' Jesus asked the boy's father. He replied, 'Since he was a little boy. The spirit often throws him into the fire or into water, trying to kill him. Have mercy on us and help us, if you can.'"

- Mark 9:17- 21, NLT

Let's take a brief moment to explore a different version together. In my opinion, the English language does not do justice in interpreting the original Greek and Hebrew texts. That's why I enjoy comparing various translations to gain a more comprehensive understanding of what the original writers meant. For example, the word "praise" is commonly found throughout the Bible, but if we look at the original Hebrew translation, it could mean "to praise with musical instruments, as if singing through them" (zamar). In another passage, the same phrase in English could be more accurately translated as "to abandon physical comfort and kneel in worship" (barach). So, when we encounter these seemingly identical phrases in

English, should we be praising God by kneeling in sacrifice or by playing an instrument skillfully? It may seem simple, but there can be conflicting interpretations if we don't understand the intention behind the original language. (There are also other Hebrew definitions for different uses of "praise", but I am by no means an expert in Hebrew!).

This section of scripture, Mark 9:22 in the KJV, depicts a father pleading desperately to Jesus for help. He cries out, "If you can do anything, have compassion on us and help us." Can't you feel the father's anguish and desperation in his words? In contrast, the NLT version presents a slightly different take on this verse. It reads, "What do you mean, 'If I can'?" Jesus asked. 'Anything is possible if a person believes.' The father immediately cried out, 'I do believe; help me overcome my unbelief!' This story may seem odd to some - why would God allow an account of someone struggling with their faith to be included in the Bible for thousands of years? Shouldn't we learn about faith from someone who never had any doubts or struggles? But that's not how the Bible works - it uses flawed and imperfect individuals to teach us about faith, including those who struggled with unbelief and doubts like this father did.

I, more than ever, could relate strongly to this father's experience. He watched his son suffer at the hands of a demonic spirit, feeling helpless to save him despite doing everything he could to help. When he came upon Jesus and begged for assistance, he so badly wanted to believe that his son could be healed. But after enduring so much pain and heartache over such a long period of time, there was still a part of him that couldn't fully trust and have faith. I understand this all too well. Before Col left for college, our family went through a crisis of faith that we thought we had resolved. Things were going well when he moved out, but when another crisis hit while he was away at school, it brought back all those old wounds and forced us to heal once again from our earlier trauma. It felt like ripping off a scab from a wound that was finally starting to heal - except now we had to wait even longer to see the final outcome of our healing process.

Chapter 4

Doubt Versus Decision

When we got the call that we could come pick up Col the next morning, I *wanted* to believe things would be good and his faith would still be solid. I knew that God had shown Himself to Col before, and I was telling myself over and over that Col would be ok. Maybe he even got to talk about his faith inside the facility and maybe, just maybe, he would come out even stronger in his faith. But underneath all that was that quiet seed of doubt. I didn't want it there - I was trying to squash and drown it with faith-building affirmations, but it was there nonetheless.

This father, too, was trying his best to believe…. but he'd been through SO MUCH with his son up to that point, that he found himself dealing with DOUBT underneath that belief. I can so relate to the desperation of this parent, trying to grasp at any amount of faith despite the underlying unbelief and doubt. And when I was at my rope's end, at a women's retreat so remote that my cell phone wouldn't even work, the Lord dropped that in my Spirit - *Faith is a decision*—knowing that I would be led to this passage in Mark about that desperate daddy. What God said to me that day was starting to make sense.

Faith *is* a decision. And it's one we have to make daily! There are times that we won't FEEL like having faith, but we have to steel ourselves to make the decision for faith regardless of what our feelings and emotions tell us at the time. The phrase the Lord gave me, "Faith is a decision" is what helped me get through my darkest doubting period - and for me, just saying that over and over to myself through those next few months helped me stay grounded about keeping my faith through that doubt.

The times when I'd realize unbelief was creeping back in, I'd have to remind myself, *Faith is a decision* and those doubts would slowly fade. In all honesty, there were plenty of times that I would have to repeatedly quote that phrase to myself - almost like a mantra:

Faith is a decision.

Faith is a decision.

Faith is a decision.

In doing so, I was gradually retraining my mind to focus on what God had told me. In Romans 12, it talks about "renewing your mind," which essentially means rewiring your brain to think in alignment with God's ways instead of the world's ways.

One of the things I love most about being in ministry is when my husband and I counsel couples before they get married. We have a pretty intense six-week curriculum we go through with the soon-to-be-wed couples, covering things from handling finances to managing in-laws.

During our premarital counseling, Jerry and I emphasize that no matter how head-over-heels in love the couple may feel at the moment or on their wedding day, there will come a time when they look at each other and do not feel jittery, butterflies-in-your-belly type of love. In fact, they might not even feel the familiar warmth of "like" for their spouse some days. It's on those days that they have to make the decision to still love regardless of how they feel on a particular day. Love is a daily decision. And so is faith.

Besides the daily decision to LOVE others even when I may not have LIKED a person, there have been times in my life (and probably will be more times) that I did something or stuck with something simply because that's what I decided to do. This was evident when I ran a 10k and achieved a personal record. Later that year, I participated in an almost 300-mile charity bike ride, despite never having done anything like it before. The training was grueling and during the event itself, I had to deal with pain and discomfort. Nonetheless, I kept going because I had made my decision. And I was determined not to let ANYONE see me giving up on my decision.

There are many decisions we all make in life that are dismissed easily, treated as minor inconveniences, while others are considered ones that we nearly stake everything upon. For some, the decision to get healthier after the first of January can be one that's easily written off, but others make that decision and a few months later, they have met every goal and have found a new lease on life.

I remember several years ago, I found myself miserable at the job I worked. There were times I would come home in tears. I did the job well. It paid the bills. But I was miserable. And like most Americans, there was no way I could afford to just quit a job because I wasn't happy there. We like to joke that I work to support my husband's preaching habit, but considering we minister at a small rural church, there is some truth to that joke. So I made a decision. I made the decision to stay where I was because it meant my family was taken care of while we were fulfilling our calling. While I did have peace about it (knowing I was in God's will helped that), there were days I was still miserable. But I had made the decision to stay there until God opened the door for something different, better or more fulfilling.

Faith operates in the same manner. We must make the conscious decision that no matter how overwhelming things may seem or what obstacles are thrown at us, regardless of our bank account balance or how we've been treated by members of the church, TODAY, I, (WE), still believe that God is in control of all things and that TODAY, He has not forgotten us. TODAY, He hears my prayers and YOUR prayers.

Father, thank You for always hearing us. Even when things go in fifty different directions and we seem to have more questions than answers, none of it takes You by surprise, and You still hold us with arms of love. Today, Lord, we choose to trust You. Today, we say "yes" to Your peace, and we say "no" to the nagging doubts that seem to try to creep into our minds repeatedly. Tomorrow will hold what it holds, but TODAY, You hold us, Lord, and we thank You and love You for that.

Psalm 5, NLT

1 O LORD, hear me as I pray; pay attention to my groaning.

2 Listen to my cry for help, my King and my God, for I pray to no one but you.

3 Listen to my voice in the morning, LORD. Each morning I bring my requests to you and wait expectantly.

4 O God, you take no pleasure in wickedness; you cannot tolerate the sins of the wicked.

5 Therefore, the proud may not stand in your presence, for you hate all who do evil.

6 You will destroy those who tell lies. The LORD detests murderers and deceivers.

7 Because of your unfailing love, I can enter your house; I will worship at your Temple with deepest awe.

8 Lead me in the right path, O LORD, or my enemies will conquer me. Make your way plain for me to follow.

9 My enemies cannot speak a truthful word. Their deepest desire is to destroy others. Their talk is foul, like the stench from an open grave. Their tongues are filled with flattery.

10 O God, declare them guilty. Let them be caught in their own traps. Drive them away because of their many sins, for they have rebelled against you.

11 But let all who take refuge in you rejoice; let them sing joyful praises forever. Spread your protection over them, that all who love your name may be filled with joy.

12 For you bless the godly, O LORD; you surround them with your shield of love.

Chapter 5

The "Doubt Is Sin" Debate

At this point, I feel that we need to take a minute to tackle up some pretty steep theological mountains together. Hang tight - we'll be doing this together! During my childhood and even into my late teens and early adulthood, I do not recall ever being told point-blank that doubt is a sin. I may have heard a well-meaning, red-faced preacher spitting it out with his alliterated and poetic points, but more than anything, I remember the feeling that we were never to present a less-than-perfect faith to the church, to the pastor or evangelist and to the Lord. When we came before the Lord, even in our bedtime prayers as children, there was a formula for our faith - and doubt had no place there.

Having faith while doubt lingers is like trying to move from one side of a cliff to another. Deep in the shadows at the bottom of that cliff was the raging river of doubt. Though I never acknowledged that river of doubt, I could hear its roar as I tried to make my way across a bridge made of my own faith. This nice, shiny, man-made bridge could take me to the other side, but as I try to get across doubt, I would find myself having to leap, sway and spin to avoid the big, gaping holes in the planks of the bridge that would plunge me deep into the river.

Of course, no one could tell from a distance that the bridge of my faith was so close to collapse. That's what the training of my southern-genteel religion did for me, helping me to portray the strong faith a "real" woman in Christ would have. My weaknesses and doubts were hidden under layers and layers of churchisms.

I now know that I'm not the only one who has found themselves at the edge of that cliff. For years, the church - especially the Western church - has quietly gaslighted its members to believe that only those dripping with perfection will enter the Kingdom of God - whether here on Earth or later in Heaven. Long before there were Instagram highlights, there were Sunday morning fashion-and-faith shows that caused women of all stations to try to present themselves as strong, perfect, Proverbs 31 women.

I realize that makes me sound incredibly disillusioned with the "big C"- church. Please know that's not the case. While there was a time that I wanted to run as far away from organized denominational religion as I could, I've since seen real, valuable, genuine acts of love *by churches*. Yes, there are many churches out there who have their priorities upside-down and put their emphasis on the opposite of what true kingdom work should look like, but there are plenty more that get it right.

Unfortunately for those of us who grew up in a church era that put more emphasis on the appearances and *visible* perfection of the saints, we have had quite the uphill climb in our imperfect faith, haven't we? That kind of picture-perfect, masked, "living out" of my faith is what caused the biggest chasm I would ever have to overcome to understand the love and acceptance I received from the Lord on a daily basis.

Why is it that for so long, for so many generations, we have given new Christians the idea that unless our faith in God is impenetrable and completely immaculate, then we must not *really* be Christians…and (gasp!) maybe we're not *really saved!?* I say that last part in a little bit of jest…a tiny bit. But that's what I dealt with...trying to reconcile if my own questioning of the existence of God really meant maybe I wasn't saved...or if I *was* saved, I was for sure "in sin".

We were taught - whether intentionally or not - that REAL faith NEVER doubts. And if you doubt, are you even saved? I felt like I had no one to go to with these questions, because I was sure I was the *only one* whose faith was so shaky. Now I know there are others who have dealt with the exact same questions, but felt there was no one to ask.

When I was at the lowest level of my faith I'd ever been (still working in the church and leading others to Christ, even!), I had to learn for myself what the Bible REALLY said (and didn't say) about questioning and doubting. I thank God that He put that phrase in my spirit, *faith is a decision*. But all my life, from my Baptist upbringing to my Pentecostal coming-of-age as a young adult, I'd ascribed to the unspoken rule that true Christians never doubted. Reconciling this decision business was throwing me for a loop.

Here's what I've learned, friend. Doubt does not cancel out salvation. And salvation will not remove every force from the enemy's arsenal that causes doubt. The two are not related, nor does one depend on the other. I encourage you to look through God's Word for verses that clarify this question for you, but for me, one of the most helpful passages has been Ephesians 1:13-14, ESV: "In him you also, when you heard the word of truth, the gospel of your salvation, and believed in him, were sealed with the promised Holy Spirit, who is the guarantee of our inheritance until we acquire possession of it, to the praise of his glory."

When we heard the Good News and believed in Him, we were sealed by the Holy Spirit. Who sealed us? God the Father. What does that mean, to be sealed? In biblical times, a *seal* was a legally binding signature! Sometimes it was a wax seal, where the signet ring of the father would be used to imprint the seal of the family crest - recognizable to all as a legally binding contract of ownership. Sometimes it was even a tattoo, inked permanently into the skin, to show who held the allegiance of the servant who bore the seal on their body.

Why would *we* need a legally binding signature? To show proper and legal *ownership*. Friend, if you have believed in Jesus, and accepted the good news of your salvation, you're His! His seal is upon you! He has sealed you with His Spirit. I do want you to note that it does not say in that scripture (or any other scripture that I've found) that if you have questions about God, that those questions nullify or void any contract between the Lord and you. He still considers me (and you, if you have believed) HIS. Like the old song from early church days, "I'm His, and He is mine!" Nothing can redefine *whose* we are once we have believed.

Still, we know even a saved person - yes, God's child - is tempted to sin. I think this brings us to these next two questions that Christians have wrestled with for centuries. Is doubt a sin? Is doubt something that we need to repent of?

I'm going to tell you, as a mama who has questioned quite literally EVERYTHING I have believed up to this point, I struggled the most with these questions. So, as I pointed out earlier, I started with the Source- the best-selling of all bestsellers: God's Word. And I'm not ashamed to say I asked for counsel on this subject from those who study the Word that I trust most, as well as reading and listening to several dozen blogs, podcasts and commentaries on the subject.

Let's first designate where in scripture we have seen doubt. Well, it might be easier to ask where in scripture did the characters have *no* doubt? Let's explore this:

Adam & Eve - In the very beginning, the serpent tempted Eve by putting a shiny fruit in front of her, but was it all about the fruit being desirable, or about doubting that God was the only supreme being worthy of the wisdom Eve thought she was missing? Remember in Genesis 3, the enemy asked Eve, "Did God *really* say that you shouldn't eat this fruit?" And by that one question, the father of lies sowed the first seeds of doubt into the heart of the matriarch of the human race.

He then continued to cultivate those seeds by telling Eve, "Oh, God didn't mean that you'd DIE!! He just meant that you'd be as smart as Him once you ate it!" (Excuse my sarcastic paraphrase.) The enemy caused Eve to not just doubt what God had really told her, but also to doubt her place - dare I say, importance - in the world that God had created for their fellowship.

We know that Eve and Adam did wind up committing a sin. Why else would God have had to follow through with the finality of banishing them from the garden that had once been their sanctuary? But I submit to you this: Their sin was never the doubt that entered their mind. Their sin was acting upon the doubt as if everything depended upon what *they* did, not what God had promised.

Let's find another doubter:

David - Reading any of David's psalms could give you the sense that this "man after God's own heart" had his own share of doubts. After all, David is one of the great men of faith mentioned in what some scholars lightly call the "Faith Hall of Fame" list in Hebrews.

But did you know there was also a time where David doubted the very call on his life? It happened just after David had the chance to kill Saul for the second time, but chose not to do so out of respect for the Lord's anointing that had at one time been placed upon Saul. Now, of course, David had that same anointing poured upon him as a boy, so he KNEW the Lord had chosen him to succeed Saul as king. But in 1 Samuel 27:1, he has himself convinced that he was surely going to die by the hand of Saul. David went from knowing God had promised that he would be king, being a conquering hero, showing strength where lesser men would give into temptation, to doubting that the Lord would preserve him until he could step into the position that he was anointed for!

John the Baptist - Oh, my! Probably one of my favorites of all the doubting surprises we find in our Christian lineage. Matthew 11:2-3, NLT states, "John the Baptist, who was in prison, heard about all the things the Messiah was doing. So he sent his disciples to ask Jesus, 'Are you the Messiah we've been expecting, or should we keep looking for someone else?'"

John. The Baptist. John, the son of Elizabeth, Mary's cousin. John, the one who would prepare the way of the Lord. John, who baptized Jesus and witnessed the dove, representing the Holy Spirit descend upon Him, and who also heard God's voice identifying Jesus as His own Son. THAT John. And he still doubted when times were dark and hard.

When he was cut off from all he knew in that prison, he started questioning the very things he had witnessed. That's right, even John had doubts.

So what did Jesus tell these men in answer to John's doubts? He didn't scold them for asking or reprimand John for questioning. Rather, He just pointed out the proof. Jesus told them to LOOK AROUND. "The blind see, the lame walk, those with leprosy are cured, the deaf hear, the dead are raised to life, and the Good News is being preached to the poor."

In other words, LOOK AROUND YOU! Don't be so consumed with the questions that you miss the evidence right in front of you!! Keep praying through the doubt and the questions - and even WITH the doubts and questions. Be honest with God, praying: *Lord, here's my doubts - and anxieties - this is what I'm having a problem with. Help me to keep my eyes where I need to be looking and not be distracted by all the sideshows vying for my attention.*

Peter - He was the disciple Jesus called out of the fishing boat and who wound up preaching the sermon that literally brought thousands to faith in one day, then spent the rest of his life building the new Christian church. Before he ever did that, Peter walked with Jesus. He slept under the same roofs, ate the same meals and went to the same temples for years. He had seen Jesus with His own eyes take a boy's lunch and feed thousands of people. He KNEW who Jesus was. But still, in the middle of that foggy night, instead of depending on his faith, I just imagine Peter let his fears enter a bit when he and the others first glimpsed the shadowy figure and wondered if they were seeing a ghost. Our Savior told him immediately not to be afraid, and comforted them with the words that He was there, with them. Even then, Peter still had to ask his Rabbi to prove Himself - "Lord, if it's really you, tell me to come to you, walking on the water." (Matthew 14:28, NLT)

Of course, we know Jesus allowed Peter his moment of proof, and reached out to welcome Peter onto the water with Him. As Peter made his way to Jesus, feeling the waves under his feet and the excitement rising in his chest, he became very aware of the heaping waves and the howling wind... and suddenly the water lapping at his feet and the gusts tousling his hair and clothes began to weigh on his new-found faith.

The thoughts of unbelief and fear increasing in his mind caused him to sink beneath those very waves he had been traipsing over to get to his Lord. After seeing and experiencing so much, he allowed fear and distractions to plant those wickedly quick-rooting seeds of doubt and he began to sink.

The Eleven Remaining Disciples- "Then the eleven disciples left for Galilee, going to the mountain where Jesus had told them to go. When they saw him, they worshiped him - but some of them doubted! Jesus came and told his disciples, 'I have been given all authority in heaven and on earth. Therefore, go and make disciples of all the nations, baptizing them in the name of the Father and the Son and the Holy Spirit. Teach these new disciples to obey all the commands I have given you. And be sure of this: I am with you always, even to the end of the age.'"

- Matthew 28:16-17, NLT

This is after Jesus had been crucified and risen from the tomb. Granted, those poor disciples had been through a lot in just a few days. But their Lord had given them instructions to go to this specific place and so they went. They obeyed those instructions, regardless of how they felt. Then Jesus showed up and some of the disciples actually doubted.... with Jesus standing right there in front of them!

The Bible goes on to tell us that they saw Jesus and *worshiped Him*. The Scripture doesn't tell us which disciples doubted and which ones worshiped. It says *they* worshiped him, then it says some of them doubted. The fact that they worshiped even while they were experiencing doubt: what if we can do the same?

Now, in all my studies on this passage and the different versions and comparisons, do you know what was missing? Jesus didn't reprimand or lecture the ones who were doubting. He didn't tell them to wait to do His work until they were men of unmoving faith. He didn't express anger or disappointment that they doubted. No, He actually commissioned them to do His work AS THEY WERE.

And before leaving, He reassured them to trust in Him, telling them that He is with them always, even up to the end of everything. He took the time to bolster their faith, never brow-beating them for having a low level of faith. He cared enough about them that His parting words were an encouragement in direct opposition of those doubts those men were feeling.

Elijah - Elijah is undeniably one of the most recognizable prophets of the Old Testament. He was probably most known for when he challenged the prophets of Baal to a sacrifice to see whose god was the real God (1 Kings 18). Each side would build an altar, sacrifice to their god, and whichever god answered by fire would prove that they were the one true god. Elijah graciously let the Baal prophets go first, and they spent *hours* calling out, crying out, chanting, flailing, flogging themselves to the point of drawing blood - all to get the attention of their god.

After several hours of no answer, Elijah started goading them a bit! "Maybe you should call out louder! Perhaps Baal is asleep! Maybe he went to the bathroom, or is daydreaming..." (Again, paraphrasing). I'm sure that went over well.

Finally, he called them over to where he was building an altar to Jehovah - our one, true God. With twelve stones, representing each of Israel's tribes, he built that altar. He dug a trench around it and put the sacrifice on it, then he called for help to get four jars of water to pour over the sacrifice, the wood and the altar. Afterwards he had them do it again. And then a *third* time - so that the trench was filled with water. Then, he prayed a simple prayer, and you guessed it, the fire of God came down, consumed the drenched sacrifice, altar and even the water from the trench!

The next verse (I Kings 18:39, NLT) says when all the people saw it, they fell face down on the ground and cried out, "The Lord - He is God! Yes, the LORD is God!" Can you imagine how Elijah felt - the euphoria of seeing the God He had served for so long answer a simple prayer in such a mighty, undeniable way?

He had all the prophets of Baal, the false god, killed. He went on to pray for rain, since they were in the middle of a long drought, and we read at the end of that chapter that a heavy wind brought a terrific rainstorm. Elijah's faith must have been on another level at that point, right? Not quite.

The very next chapter tells us of Ahab telling his wife, Jezebel, what had happened, and she was not happy with someone else getting attention. So she sent a message to Elijah, threatening to kill him.

After all he'd been through and seen, her threat really got to the prophet, so much so that he went running scared into the wilderness. It was there under a tree, in his depression, Elijah, the most well-known prophet of the Old Testament, fell into a season of doubt. He went from a literal mountaintop experience to a place of fear and depression which led straight to thoughts and feelings of doubt.

Seeing the *one true prophet of God* go through what I feel like I went through with my son, was so very enlightening to me. I had gone from feeling like everything was right and running smoothly to having the foundation of our family's faith literally crumble beneath our feet. Reading about what happened to Elijah, Peter and the others helped me to understand that contrary to what the enemy wanted me to believe, I was NOT ALONE in my doubts!

There's so many more examples of people of great faith in the Bible who dealt with doubt at inexplicable times! If even these spiritual superstars can experience times of doubt woven into their tapestry of faith, why do we allow ourselves to feel disingenuous, counterfeit or less-than if we have (and dare admit to having) times of doubt? Why are we made to feel that our faith has to be perfect? Why must we feel that we can't be good Christians and bring others to the faith, if other people knew that we struggle with doubt, and sometimes questioned our faith?

Throughout the Bible, what was the Lord's response to those questions and doubts? Well, not a single doubter was damned to Hell because of it. For Eve and Adam, they did have some consequences to the actions, the real sin, that they chose *after* they doubted. But not for the questions or the act of doubting itself. For David, Elijah, Peter and the others, our Lord answered questions, asked one or two of His own and used those times as a loving shepherd and mentor would use any "teachable moment" in their loved ones' lives. In fact, in Adam and Eve's case, the Lord still addressed the teachable moment and spoke to the "doubt" questions before the repercussions from their sinful actions took place.

In exploring all this, I had a couple of big questions of my own that I would imagine anyone else might have: *What if I'm just trying to make myself feel better about all this, and doubting and questioning really does mean I'm not a good Christian?*

Does anyone else question themselves this much? I had several moments where I thought to myself that all this "Faith is a decision" business was just me, trying to make myself feel better. But then, I was reminded that HE, My God, is the One that told me faith is a decision to begin with. To be honest, there's no way I would have thought of that on my own, especially in the frame of mind I had been in for so long with all we were going through with my son and my own faith.

Sometimes, we have to remind ourselves over and over of what the Lord has told us. This has definitely been one of those times. Breaking the habit of "perfect" in my faith has required that I dig deeper than tradition and cliches. In my digging, I had to remind myself pretty often that I had heard from the Lord, and nothing would change that. Still, those thoughts didn't die easily: *But I still feel like it's bad that I doubt. Like I need to apologize or repent for doubting. If it's not a sin, why do I feel like I need to repent?*

I think the clarity of the solution is going to be found in how doubt is classified. When I was wrestling over this myself, I found myself analyzing the hows and whys of all these questions, and my husband who is more well-studied in the Word than most long-term ministers I've met, reminded me of this passage:

"Therefore, since we are surrounded by such a huge crowd of witnesses to the life of faith, let us strip off every weight that slows us down, especially the sin that so easily trips us up. And let us run with endurance the race God has set before us."

- Hebrews 12:1, NLT

Doubting and questioning may not be sin, but they can definitely weigh on us, holding us back and slowing us down. The Lord bringing that scripture to my and my husband's attention at just the right time caused me to realize that it's not just sins we have to be careful of. It's also the weights that hold us back. In fact, the Message Bible calls it "spiritual fat". Isn't that such a vivid image? Just like a runner in training can be held back from running as fast as they'd like because of the extra weight they are carrying, so can the spiritual fat of unnecessary legalism and man-made rules also hold us back from the depth and distance God is calling us to so we can go deeper in our relationship with Him.

My doubts definitely held me back. I wanted to believe, I wanted to have faith that was unmoving, but I was held back from that *because* of the questions and doubts I had - and the guilt associated with it. While I don't totally ascribe to doubt being a sin, I wholeheartedly agree that it can hold us back from moving forward.

Just like when we are in a relationship with a spouse, there are things that we do that can cause a stumbling block in our relationships. Things like infidelity or abuse might absolutely damage the relationship beyond repair. But if I were to repeatedly leave my car's gas tank on empty until I knew my husband was about to drive it so that HE would have to be the one to fill up the tank, even knowing that it gets on my husband's nerves when I do that, that wouldn't necessarily be enough to cause irreparable damage to the relationship but it would be an irritating distraction to him. It might cause a bumpy spot in the marriage; because I know that would get under his skin, and because I love him and want our relationship to weather all the tough times, I would apologize because of my love for him. Thankfully, our relationship is stronger than an empty gas tank, but an apology would *enrich* the relationship.

That's how I see the feeling of needing to apologize or repent for doubting and questioning God. Yes, I believe it's ok to doubt and question. And I believe it is well and good to apologize, repent and try not to doubt and question - because it helps the RELATIONSHIP we have with the Father to remain truthful, and helps us to recognize that we are so very fallible.

But what about the verse in James that talks about being double-minded? I've heard many, many Christians quoting James 1:6 as a means of teaching that to doubt is a sin, and is therefore, wrong. I'll probably always continue to dig into studying this passage, but let me share with you what I've found so far.

It's important to realize the context of all scriptures. James was writing to Jewish Christian people several years after Christ's death. They had been scattered, due to the persecution of early Jewish Christians. James, who did not necessarily follow Christ when He was there walking the earth, likely became a believer after Christ's death and resurrection, like Paul did. And he saw that there were a lot of things happening in the early church that just weren't becoming of Jewish Christians. So much so, that it was hard to tell a Jewish Christian from any other person or faith in that region because they didn't live out the holy standard the Lord had given them.

I love recommending the book of James to new or rededicated believers. It's a short read, the language is super easy to understand for the most part and James tackles the practical, day-to-day kind of questions most Christians have at some point in their walks.

In the first chapter, he purposefully speaks to the question of faith, specifically how to have faith when you're going through hard times while encouraging the reader to ask God for the things we need like wisdom. Then James goes on to instruct readers to ask God for what we desire in faith, believing and not wavering. Some versions actually say "believing and not doubting."

I love how Rev. E. G. Punchard, D.D. in the Ellicott Commentary for English Readers communicated the imagery of the believer *wavering* in their faith in this verse.

> "…Like storm-beaten sailors, the doubtful are "carried" up to heaven and down again to the deep; their soul melteth away because of the trouble (Psalm 107:26). And who can describe the terror, even of the faithful, in those hours of darkness when the face of the Lord is hidden; when, as with the disciples of old, the ship is in the midst of the sea, tossed with the bitter waves. Nevertheless, the raging wind will clear the heavens soon from clouds, and by the radiance of the peaceful moon we too may behold our Helper near—the Lord Jesus walking on the sea—and if He come into the ship the storm must cease."

I'm not sure how much better someone can describe the desperation of someone going through a doubting season after a time of full faith. "Terror" is an apt emotion for those times when I realized that I could not fully say I believed the Lord was there for me. Terror not just of being alone, but of living a lie. Of knowing that I was never more unqualified to be who I claimed to be than at those moments. Or at least feeling that way. Then, dealing with the times of reassuring of my faith, to top off those waves where I could see and feel the warmth of His presence again, only to find myself plummeting back into the depths of doubt again. The terror, panic and hopelessness would come back.

After reading that commentary on wavering in James 1:6, I wanted to get to the root of the original Greek translation to see how it compared. So, I sought The Strong's Exhaustive Concordance. (I was first introduced to this massive resource before the internet made it so user-friendly. If you haven't found the treasure of this resource, and you enjoy word history and etymology as much as I do, all you have to do is an internet search to find many links and even some online tutorials for best using this concordance.)

In this passage, where the phrase "doubting nothing" or "not wavering" as some translations state, the Greek word *diakrinó* is used. Traditionally, this word was defined as "to judge, to distinguish", and can be used in a phrase like "I distinguish...", "I judge..." or even "I doubt...." or "I hesitate..." The same Greek word *diakrinó* that is used in James 1:6 is also used in Acts 10:19-20, NLT:"Meanwhile, as Peter was puzzled over the vision, the Holy Spirit said to him, "Three men have come looking for you. Get up, go downstairs, and go with them without hesitation. Don't worry, for I have sent them." And again that same word *diakrinó* is used in Romans 4:20: "Abraham never wavered in believing God's promise. In fact, his faith grew stronger, and in this he brought glory to God."

So perhaps a better understanding of James' use of *diakrinó* might be, "But when you ask, you must believe and not *hesitate* [doubt], because the one who hesitates [doubts] is like a wave of the sea, blown and tossed by the wind."

This comically reminds me a bit of playing card games with my daddy as a girl, when he'd tell me, "If you think long, you think wrong." He did not like waiting on us to figure out our next moves, wavering back and forth on which cards to play or discard.

When we doubt, when we question, there's quite a bit of hesitation to be had, isn't there? Wavering back and forth, wondering if this is the right answer or that is; wondering if the Lord is listening or not; wondering if it is even okay for me to ask this or not; wondering if He's even there…. or not.

On the other hand, when we've made a decision, there's no hesitation. We have already chosen our response before the question is even posed.

Remember, *faith is a decision.* In that decision, there's no hesitancy. Our doubts and questioning fade away as we become resolute in our belief and free from unsure questioning and from paralysis over analysis. Within the decision to have faith is freedom!

Chapter 6

Worshiping In the Darkness

Elisabeth Elliot was a wonderful Christian author, speaker and minister. Her first husband, Jim Elliot, was brutally killed in 1956 while attempting to make missionary contact with the Auca people of eastern Ecuador. She later spent two years as a missionary to the same tribe who killed her husband. If ANYONE knows about keeping the faith, I think it would be her.

In her book, *Secure in the Everlasting Arms,* she wrote this about faith:

"Faith is a decision. It is not a deduction from the facts around us. We could not look at the world today and logically conclude that God loves us. It doesn't always look as though He does. Faith is not an instinct. It certainly is not a feeling - feelings don't help much when you're in the lion's den or hanging on a wooden cross. Faith is not inferred from the happy way things work. It is an act of the will, a choice, based on the Unbreakable Word of God who cannot lie, and who showed us what love and obedience and sacrifice mean, in the person of Jesus Christ."

Wow. Let that sink in: FAITH is based NOT ON US or anything that we can or cannot do, but on the UNBREAKABLE WORD OF GOD. God, who CANNOT lie. God, the most consistent part of our entire existence.

When I say "Faith is a decision," it may sound simple, but that's because our faith is not based on our own actions or flimsy emotions, but on God's love. Depending on ourselves to manufacture our faith won't work. We can't sing enough or praise enough, volunteer enough or even (gasp!) give enough to make our faith strong. We have to depend on God, because His actions are the only ones that are trustworthy, steady and unchanging.

That doesn't mean we don't put forth some effort to enter His presence. Sometimes, worshiping takes effort on our part. Even when we don't feel like worshiping, we can still do it. Worship takes effort, especially when we don't feel like it. It's not always easy to push through distractions and dryness to worship. But when we do, it can bring such joy and delight in His presence. And in those dark moments of life, we are reminded of who our faith truly depends on. Unfortunately, sometimes we focus more on the feeling of delight rather than depending on God.

We can learn a lot about worshiping in dark shadows and truly depending on God from a well-known patriarch of the Old Testament, Job.

Job was a respected man in his community. Successful in the eyes of his peers by any measure: his wealth, his family, his faith. He had a reputation of being a faithful, devout man. Then he lost his crops, his livestock, his servants…and even all ten of his children. All in the same day.

In fact, the Bible tells us in Job that when Job got the first news of his loss, before that messenger had finished speaking, another one came to tell him of more bad news. And before that one finished, another messenger came with more bad news. One on top of the other…Can you imagine? Having no time at all to process the horrible loss of your livelihood and possessions, then to be told that your children have all been killed. The Bible tells us Job tore his robe and shaved his head, and I don't think anyone would blame him.

But what he did next may shock you. Job 1:20-21 says: "Job stood up and tore his robe in grief. Then he shaved his head and fell to the ground to worship. He said, "I came naked from my mother's womb, and I will be naked when I leave. The LORD gave me what I had, and the LORD has taken it away. Praise the name of the LORD!"

Job chose to still worship, in spite of the worst darkness of his life. Even when things got worse (after losing his health), when others told him he should just curse God and die, he still chose to worship God. Wow!

Another example of worshiping and serving in dark shadows comes from the New Testament in the testimony of Paul. Paul wound up authoring most of the major books in the New Testament after his conversion - as well as building and leading the first churches of the Christian faith...all while he was imprisoned, enduring cruel acts of persecution because of the very faith in which he was discipling others.

Paul even wrote to the Corinthians that he and Timothy had endured so much that they thought they were going to die:

"We think you ought to know, dear brothers and sisters, about the trouble we went through in the province of Asia. We were crushed and overwhelmed beyond our ability to endure, and we thought we would never live through it."

- 2 Corinthians 1:8, NLT

But through all the turmoil, the persecution, the physical pain and problems, Paul chose to worship no matter how dark a place he was at the moment.

Still need another example? How about one that may be a little less well-known than Paul or Job? In fact, this person was likely overlooked on a daily basis, but Jesus noticed her sacrifice of worship when no one else did.

Jesus was sitting in the temple, watching as people came to give their offering. The more wealthy people gave substantially, and I'm sure some even made quite the show of their giving. But Jesus saw a widow woman slip two mites into the offering, and he knew she was sacrificing more than the wealthy ones giving their offerings (see Mark 12 and Luke 21).

This woman was a widow, which meant she had no viable source of income or even a respectable standing in society after her husband's death. Yet she chose to still worship with what she could, when she could, even in the middle of her dark season as a widowed woman in Biblical times. She chose to depend on the Lord as she worshiped.

Maybe you've been *delighting* in God and enjoying those brief glimpses of light His presence can bring, but not *depending* on Him. Don't make depending on God an act of desperation, make it an act of decision. Faith is a decision. A deliberate decision.

Chapter 7

Suit Up in Armor

When Col was just a preschooler, he made the decision to live for Jesus - and shortly after that became interested in getting baptized to make his decision public. We sat with him and made sure he understood what it was all about on his own little level, and he was so excited!

Baptism Day came, and my husband was understandably a bit emotional, since this time, he was getting to baptize his own son. The whole church was excited, and could you blame them? My boy was such a cutie, and he was so excited about his baptism!

When the time came, Jerry was waiting for Col in the baptism pool at the end of service. Col was stepping carefully down each of the steps getting into the water. He was so little the water would have probably gone over his nose if he stood flatfooted on the bottom, so he tippy-toed a bit and Jerry was there to hold his hand and keep him steady.

But then, little Col must have realized just how deep that water was and that it was actually going to go over his head. That little, adorable ball of energy freaked out to the point that he *climbed up his Daddy's torso* to get out of the water! He was hanging onto Jerry's shoulders and would not come down. He truly was scared - the poor guy was crying and almost hysterical, so Jerry wound up having to get out of the water with Col and we worked to calm him down.

A week later, we refilled the baptistry and had another Baptism Day at the end of service. This time, Col was prepared. He had really wanted to be baptized, but had a fear of going under the water...without his goggles (which he called "gobbles" in his little 4-year-old voice). So, before he went in the water, he suited up with his "gobbles" and faced that water. I'm telling you, it was like another kid stepped into the water, he was so confident! The only difference between the two weeks' attempts was Col's readiness. In his mind, he needed the correct equipment to be safe in that water. He had to get suited up!

How much easier would our life be if we could walk into our "scary" or even questionable situations - confident, suited up and ready for the fight? Friend, we have already been given everything we need for that! We are reminded of this in Ephesians when Paul is instructing the early church to make sure they put on the full armor of God. I've heard so many preachers and teachers over the years preach every possible angle of this passage. But as I've learned over the years, when we avail ourselves to God's Word, sometimes the parts that we've read and re-read a thousand times take on a whole new life for us when we most need it.

In this case, I was reading over this passage when the verbiage of Ephesians 6 just jumped off the page at me. In the 16th verse, where Paul mentions the shield of FAITH, several versions tell us to "take" the shield of faith:

"Therefore take up the whole armor of God, that you may be able to withstand in the evil day, and having done all, to stand firm. Stand therefore, having fastened on the belt of truth, and having put on the breastplate of righteousness, and, as shoes for your feet, having put on the readiness given by the gospel of peace. In all circumstances take up the shield of faith, with which you can extinguish all the flaming darts of the evil one; and take the helmet of salvation, and the sword of the Spirit, which is the word of God, praying at all times in the Spirit, with all prayer and supplication."

- Ephesians 6:13-16, ESV

This kind of caught me right in the middle of skimming past it. I noticed that this shield of faith was the first piece of God's armor that required we actually do something *presently* with it. Follow me here. Notice that, in the verses right before, Paul teaches us that we are to make sure we're clothed in the armor of God so that we will be able to "withstand" (or as my favorite phrasing puts it, to "stand, therefore"). Then he starts mentioning the pieces that we should already have in place before we stand: the breastplate of righteousness, belt of truth and the essential battle-protective shoes of the good news of God's peace.

Our righteousness (right-standing in God's eyes), our dependence on the truth and our protection we receive from God's peace will already be in place by the time we get to the point where Paul is telling us what to do next. He tells us that after all of the suiting up, NOW (above all, in all circumstances, in every situation) we must *take up* the shield of faith.

Our righteousness through God, His peace and His truth, may not need to be continually reapplied or re-decided, as the case may be. But our faith, that heavy, yet strong shield of faith, has to be taken up in EVERY situation. Every time there is a decision to be made, a question to be asked or a doubt to be conquered, faith must be taken up *each time*.

Here's the thing: you can't "take up" something by accident. You have to make the decision to grasp it, lifting it higher into position to ward off the "fiery darts" of the enemy with intention. We DECIDE to take up the shield of faith. Not only that, but I've learned that the original Greek etymology of that word "take" infers repetition, as in having to take up the shield of faith over and over again. That's why the writer mentioned that in every situation, in all circumstances, the shield must be picked up and put to use. We have to decide DAILY to have faith.

When we wake up, knowing that the situation that left us nearly sleepless the night before hasn't changed one bit, we CHOOSE to pick up our faith again. Not because we are the ones so faithful, but because God is and always has been. When you are running late to work, get a flat tire and find out when you finally get to work - late - that you've been looked over yet again for another promotion, you *choose* to pick up your shield of faith again. Yes, you're feeling overwhelmed and underpaid, and it's ok to feel that. But you still pick up your shield of faith because you know that even though you feel those things, it doesn't change that God is still faithful. Even in this very unfair and unfaithful world, we pick up that shield of faith, and as we do, we are reminded again that GOD IS FAITHFUL.

That shield Paul talks about in the letter to the Ephesians wasn't just a decorative ceremonial shield, there for the looks. This shield was a battle shield, and it was built to purposefully last through hard battles. History[1] tells us that Roman battle shields were around 2 feet by 4 feet, and were made from wood that had been covered with leather. The size and durability of the wood and leather would effectively shield the soldier's entire body from fiery arrows, as well as the sword.

Can you imagine how heavy that shield was? Some historians believe it would normally weigh as much as 22 pounds! In fact, the soldiers would actually soak the shield in water before battle so that the wet leather and wood would better protect them from any fire from arrows launched. The weight of the shield combined with the wet leather made the shield a great weapon for defense,

---

[1] Ancient Pages. Oct. 2024. A. Sutherland, 2009. https://www.ancientpages.com/2018/10/01/fascinating-ancient-history-of-roman-shields/

but simultaneously made a great offensive weapon if the soldiers needed to push through an enemy line.

When we think of the Roman shield, or *scutum*[2], we often overlook a crucial aspect: the design on each side. You see, the Romans knew that as strong as a single soldier was, the entire army of soldiers unified could very well be an unstoppable force. So the Romans built their shields with interlocking pieces on either side of the shield, so that the soldiers could create an impenetrable wall. They'd link their shields together and as they held them in position, usually angled high to protect their upper bodies and heads, the line of soldiers would begin to march forward, performing what was called a phalanx advance against the enemy.

Their interlocked shields created a wall of protection so that they literally could march right up to the enemy lines. They'd be protected the whole way, and then they would strike the enemy with their swords through the phalanx, push the enemies back, and in most instances, conquer their foes simply by linking and fighting *together*.

Friend, it is not a coincidence that Paul used this type of shield to teach us about the armor of

---

[2] UNRV. Oct. 2024. UNRV.com, 2024. https://www.unrv.com/military/scutum.php

God. Just like those Roman armies, we are much stronger and much better protected from the enemy's attacks when we link our shields of faith with other Christian brothers and sisters. Just as taking up your own shield of faith has to be an intentional decision, we have to *deliberately* decide to take up our own shield to intentionally link up with our fellow soldiers' shields.

Now, when I was in the middle of my faith crisis, not knowing if I even believed anymore all that I had been preaching for years, the thought of intentionally reaching out and finding someone with stronger faith (or any faith at all), attempting to link up to help me fight this battle would flood me with such strong, conflicting emotions. On one hand, there'd be a sense of relief, almost hope. Perhaps there was someone out there who could support me and help me make sense of my doubts. Maybe their prayers would reach God when mine felt ineffective. Maybe just knowing that someone else had faith would bring joy back into my life.

But then, contradicting and shadowing that hope was a form of dread. Dread, embarrassment and the sense of being a failure. How could I reach out to link up with someone's faith? What would they think? How could I be in the position I was in, and admit to having faith issues? Why would anyone want to help me?

When I felt like I had no other options, I finally confided in a close friend. Everything that had been weighing on me for so long came pouring out, and even though part of me wanted to hold back and minimize my struggles, I laid it all out for her. I don't remember much more about that day, but before speaking to her, I was at my worst, feeling like I could barely breathe from the weight of my anxiety. After she prayed for me, it was like a weight had been lifted and I could breathe freely again. In the following months, Kate and her husband continued to support us, even connecting us with someone who had experience with similar struggles.

As I delved deeper into my study of the shield of faith, I realized that joining my weathered shield with my friends' stronger ones was a turning point in my situation. My son's struggles didn't magically disappear, and my own doubts and imperfect faith weren't suddenly resolved. What did happen was I felt the support of another strong mama-warrior, bolstering my own shield of faith as we fought together. She would call to check on me, providing a much-needed boost while our shields were linked. When I faced setbacks in my son's agnosticism and lifestyle, I could text her for prayers and we would move forward together.

The rugged functionality of the old Roman shields serves as a perfect analogy for navigating life's shadows with our fellow believers. Our God, in His infinite wisdom, created us to function better together than alone. I firmly believe that one of the enemy's most effective tactics is isolating us and convincing us that we are alone in our struggles, that no one will understand. And I have fallen prey to this tactic before. But thankfully, we have a powerful weapon to combat it - our shield of faith. We can use it on our own, but when joined with someone else who shares the same faith, even if it may be weak at times, we can defeat the enemy together. This is how we were meant to wage this battle.

There's one more thing I'd like you to remember about taking up your shield. Sometimes we have to choose *multiple* times a day to pick up that shield of faith again. That's right. Why is that? Because those fiery darts that the enemy launches at us are meant to hurt us. And sometimes the impact of those weapons, especially when they come over and over again, causes us to loosen our grip on our shield of faith just enough that the next incoming blast dislodges the frenzied grip we have on the shield, and it falls, crashing to the ground.

At that moment, we have to make the choice to pick up the shield *again*. Yes, we'd already picked it up, but sometimes life throws fiery obstacles that make us lose our grip! And the fiery darts *will* come. No matter where we are in life, what station we might hold or what level of faith we think we have that day, there will be attacks from the enemy. Even Jesus Himself told us that in this life we will have trouble. He didn't say that only those of little faith will have trouble (John 16:33). He didn't say that the "REAL" Christians would always have it easy. He didn't even say that he'd make the troubles disappear.

Friend, we shouldn't let ourselves feel less of a Christian when these fiery darts come. Just because they come, does NOT mean you've done something wrong in your walk with the Lord. Doubt can be like those fiery darts; we need to know there will be times of doubt, but just because we have them doesn't make us "less than" in God's eyes.

The reason we are told to suit up with the whole armor of God in the first place is so we can withstand the evil (fiery darts) in our days. We must do what we know to do, repeatedly. Every day. In every circumstance, we take it up. And then, STAND. Notice Paul didn't say "then get up and stand." He said "stand therefore". You're already standing! Just keep it up.

You know what makes a successful, strong and faithful Christian? One who lasts. One who stands, despite everything being thrown at them. God knows us well enough to know we can't last on our own, so He has given us exactly what we need to be able to stand therefore and last. We just have to make the *decision* to keep picking it up.

Sounds so easy, doesn't it? Some of us can quickly make decisions and never question them. Still others I KNOW are sitting there saying, "How am I supposed to just DECIDE and then suddenly everything will be OK? Just deciding gets rid of my doubt? Right." I get you, friend. In the next chapter, I'll give you some things to remember when you feel your faith is becoming weak and your doubts are becoming insurmountable.

Chapter 8

Faith Despite Doubt

We have some friends who keep us updated pretty regularly on their little ones' concepts of all things God, church and family related - especially the more comical ones. One afternoon in the car, the middle brother pipes up, "You know, God is like slime."

His little sister, with her *threenager* attitude says, "NO, he's not, DJ!" DJ quickly calls for his mama's validation: "Yes, He is! Right, mama???" Mama was not quite sure where he was heading with this, so she just said, "Ummmm, I'm not sure what you mean, DJ." Then DJ clears everything up with all his wisdom and says, "I meeaannnnnnnn.... God IS like slime! His love just sticks to us and we can't get it off!"

Our faith (or lack thereof) doesn't affect God OR His Power. It only AFFECTS US. Did you know God is not intimidated one bit by what we think of Him! Truth: we could think He's the best thing ever - and He will love us. Also truth: We could think He's the biggest waste of time - and He will love us. We could think His followers are brainwashed and there's no way He exists - and He will still love us. Please understand: humanity's OPINION of God has no bearing on WHO HE IS.

He's bigger, better, stronger and greater than all that! Let's look at the example of Job in the Bible. Job actually questioned God's wisdom (to be honest, I understand Job here) and the Lord answered Job starting in Job 38, and He didn't finish addressing Job until the end of Chapter 41!!

I don't know why or how the Creator of all things can stoop so low as to love an indecisive, doubting, shaky sinner like me. But HERE is what I DO know:

God is still God, whether we believe He is or not.

He still heals, whether we believe He heals or not.

He still saves, whether we believe He does or not.

He still comforts, whether we feel the comfort or not.

He still moves, whether we see Him move or not.

He still delivers, whether we see the deliverance or not.

He still HEARS US.... WHETHER WE THINK HE DOES OR NOT.

My faith does not affect who God is OR His love for me because faith really shouldn't be about us - it's about how constant, how dependable, how trustworthy our God is.

And that brings me to my next point: we can still pray, even when we have doubts and questions! For those, like me, who thought *the presence of doubt* must mean I'm a lesser Christian, hear me again: Doubt does not mean you've backslid or committed some grievous sin. God is not going to STOP listening to you just because you're having doubts!

Christian author Ed Dobson wrote, "Faith is not the ABSENCE of doubt." Friend, having faith doesn't mean you'll never doubt. In fact, some would say you really can't have faith without a little doubt! Something you couldn't doubt, wouldn't require FAITH. That's the point! Therefore, you CAN pray even when you have doubts.

In my journey, I think this was one of the hardest concepts to wrap my brain around. As a pastor's wife, minister and a Christian most of my life, the fact that I was doubting the very thing I'd committed my life to promoting seemed like such a reversal of what I had built (or thought I had) in my life and my family. I felt like such a hypocrite.

But the fact that I felt that way didn't change a single thing about the way God the Father feels about me. Like the slime my friend's adorable little boy referenced, God's love sticks!

Chapter 9
Faith = Trust + Confidence

I found this equation in a devotional that I happen to come across right in the middle of that trying season. Evangelist Joyce Meyer says, "Faith is a decision we make about where we are going to put our trust."

If faith seems to be too big of a mountain to climb today, let's focus instead on just starting to *trust*. For me, even though I was doubting so very much, I still trusted that if God was who He said He was, then He would do what He said He would do. I still trusted that He knew better than me. I just didn't feel that He would do those things *for* me and my family.

This takes us to probably one of the most well-known verses about trust and feelings in the Bible:

"Trust in the Lord with all your heart; do not depend on your own understanding. Seek his will in all you do, and he will show you which path to take."

- Proverbs 3:5-6, NLT

In other words, trust in the Lord - don't trust yourself or your feelings. Feelings lie. TRUST GOD, who never changes, who cannot lie. Trust HIM!

Back when Jerry and I came back from our honeymoon, bright-eyed and ready to work for the Lord, we had a message on our answering machine (yes, that long ago) from a pastor nearly two hours away who wanted to interview Jerry for what would be his first full-time, paid ministerial position. We were elated! After the interview, he got hired!

Our home church was so proud too. Jerry was kind of the church baby; before sending us off, they had us stand in service and prayed over us to be "set forth" into ministry. They even hosted a covered dish supper for us to honor the time Jerry had spent in ministry there, growing up and into adulthood. Then we moved two hours away from everything we knew and set to work in this small, agricultural community church, building the youth group and working in the music department.

Jerry would go to the public high school each week to have lunch with "our" kids, and even helped to start a Christian student-led lunchtime devotional that outgrew the classroom they met in. Within a few weeks, the youth events we hosted after football games had grown to over 70 kids. Then just a mere three months into this assignment, the pastor called Jerry to let him know that night the church council would be meeting to determine if they were going to keep Jerry on as a youth and music minister or fire him.

Jerry was blindsided, understandably. He asked if he could be there to defend himself or answer any questions and was told it probably wouldn't be a good idea. So, three months into our first pastoral position, we were "fired" (though we still don't know the reason to this day). To add insult to injury, they asked us to stick around for another month and not tell anyone that we were leaving yet. Having no options, we did as we were asked, and soon found ourselves having to move back home.... to live with HIS parents in their house as newlyweds.

Walking into his home church those first few services after we came back home was hard. REALLY hard. One Sunday morning, I was sitting in our usual spot on the front row while Jerry played the drums for the worship team (always the servant). I remember so well, standing there during worship with everyone around me singing and raising their hands in worship. But I didn't *feel* like worshiping. In fact, I remember just silently complaining in my heart to God, *Father I don't feel like being here. I don't feel like worshiping.* I felt like everyone was pitying us, thinking we had messed up somehow and talking about us. I *definitely* didn't feel like raising my hands in worship. And that was when God clearly spoke to me (the first time in my life that I knew that God spoke directly to me) and said, *Daughter, how you feel has no bearing on WHO I Am.*

It was then, as a young, fresh-faced newlywed that I decided no matter whether I *felt* like it or not, I would never squander an opportunity to worship God for who He is! I think that's why, even in my darkest doubting times during the experience with my son, I still tried my best to get into worship and praise when I could. Even though, Lord knows, I sure didn't *feel like it.*

I'd learned not to trust myself or my feelings. I'm someone that tends to be ruled way too much by those lying emotions. So if I can't trust myself, I have to make the decision to trust God. Not because I feel like it, but because He has proven time and time again that He CAN be trusted. And not just to me - and not just to you, whether you see it yet or not, but to thousands of generations through the ages.

Trusting in Him despite our feelings may seem a bit disingenuous at times, but you'll find out as I did, that trust in God (even when we don't feel like it) will breed confidence. Not confidence in self, but in Him; some people call it God-fidence! I'm talking about the confidence that God is good and He will do what He said He will do!

How does that happen? Now remember we're not talking about building *big* faith here...we're starting small, building one piece at a time. We are just TRUSTING God to start with. The more you trust God, the more you'll start seeing His promises kept. You'll see that *this* family had an unexpected blessing with their finances, and *this* mama had a promise kept with her child's health, and *that* brother just got a long-awaited promotion, and *that* sister was delivered from a meth addiction, and *this* prodigal is on the way home. You'll see the goodness of God working in ways you would have overlooked before. Your focus will start to change.

Think about someone you trust immensely. Maybe it's a parent, a grandparent, a neighbor who stepped in when no one else would. When you are with that person that you have come to trust, you're not on pins and needles, waiting for the next blow to come, are you? You're not sitting there with breath held tight, trying to make sure nothing sets them off....no! You can be in a state of peace around them, breathing deeply in the calming effect that real trust will bring to your soul. You ultimately have confidence that they have your best interests at heart, no matter what else you are going through.

I believe that is how confidence in God grows. You begin with trusting God, because let's be honest, He really hasn't failed us at all, has He? Then you start gaining confidence that maybe, just maybe God will keep all His promises to you and your children. His timing may be different than what you'd prefer, but I trust that in the waiting, He'll be fulfilling other promises, like giving you strength to last (see Isaiah 40:31) and providing your child protection from the attacks of the enemy (see Proverbs 14:26).

And if you want to build your confidence even more, you can just turn to these 1,696 pages I have in my Bible - and read how TIME AFTER TIME, our God was a promise keeper - for

GENERATIONS! Because He has proven Himself time and time again, we can have confidence that He will keep working that way! We have confidence that HE WILL DO WHAT HE SAID HE WILL DO.

Think about it. How much more peaceful and calm do you feel when looking back at how He has kept His Word versus the way we feel when we try to figure out how or *even if* He will keep His Word for what we are facing right now? It reminds me of a quote by Lysa TerKeurst: "Tracing God's hand of faithfulness from the past is so much more calming than trying to predict the future."

When I look back and start remembering how God has been so faithful to me, through the big and the small things, I noticeably feel lighter! I would think back to a time when me and my husband were trying to conceive, and the Lord gave a Word to a friend of mine to remind me to thank God every day for the baby He would give me, even though it had been years of trying. Because the baby *was* coming. And roughly about three months later, we found out we were finally pregnant.

I would always recall how my husband and I, coming from less than ideal family backgrounds when it came to marital bliss, were fortunate enough to have a strong and loving relationship that exceeded any dreams I had as a child.

I would remember the time I was stressing about Col's college choices, and very distinctly felt God's voice telling me that HE had a plan for Col and I was going to have to let go of my plans. The feeling of having the oxygen pulled out of my lungs because the presence of God was so real right then somehow giving me dueling feelings of intense reverence, helping me to understand true fear of the Lord and an immediate sense of peace that He already had all of it figured out.

Let's revisit that story from Mark 9, the one where Jesus delivered that precious son at the request of the doubting father. We *know* that Jesus delivered that boy. The people there could SEE what had happened; they had no problem trusting when they saw that!

Do you think that Jesus would have been surprised to learn that the father had doubts underneath that thin layer of faith? Of course not! But what if the miracle Jesus performed for that father wasn't just about delivering his son, but about building- even resurrecting- the father's faith?

See, I have come to believe - *to trust* - that HE CARES that much about the doubters. I have confidence that He cares *that much* about those of us that are hanging onto our faith by a thread. And with that, I have come to have faith that what He has done for others for generations upon generations, He will do for me too. He's just that good and He never changes.

He KNOWS that there will be times that it seems like we have more doubt than faith, but still He promises to give us strength when we need it. In fact, this passage from The Message Bible says:

"Why would you ever complain, O Jacob, or, whine, Israel, saying, 'God has lost track of me. He doesn't care what happens to me?' Don't you know anything? Haven't you been listening? God doesn't come and go. God lasts. He's Creator of all you can see or imagine. He doesn't get tired out, doesn't pause to catch his breath. And he knows everything, inside and out. He energizes those who get tired, gives fresh strength to dropouts. For even young people tire and drop out, young folk in their prime stumble and fall. But those who wait upon God get fresh strength. They spread their wings and soar like eagles, They run and don't get tired, they walk and don't lag behind."

- Isaiah 40:27-31, MSG

Again, it comes down to this: Faith = Trust + Confidence. If we can focus FIRST on just trusting HIM more than we do ourselves and our feelings and confidently wait on Him to do what He said He would, then our faith will naturally grow! We have to remember: He's good. He's unchanging, always steady. He lasts! That means His end is handled! We just have to make the *decision* to have faith in Him –by trusting Him first, and then being confident that He'll do what He said He would do. That's when faith comes in.

Chapter 10:

God Loves Doubters

Time for self-introspection. How many of you have had some REALLY LOW levels of faith recently? How many of you doubted so much that you were ashamed to even tell someone else? Let me just put you at ease- you are NOT THE ONLY ONE!

From the beginning of time, there have been people who had to make the choice to lean into what God had said, instead of depending on how they felt. I think some of the most well-known characters in the Bible to live this out were probably the three Hebrew boys we heard about so long ago in Sunday School: Shadrach, Meshach and Abednego. There's even been songs written about their adventure in the furnace.

These young men were kidnapped from their native land and brought into Babylon in captivity. They were given new, Babylonian names (the ones we know them as), and trained to work as Babylonians in the king's court. So, they were in a foreign land, stripped of their Hebrew names they had always been known as, and forced to learn and work alongside the very people who conquered and kidnapped them.

One day, King Nebuchadnezzar decreed that when the music was played on certain instruments, everyone was to bow down and worship the golden statue the king had placed for that purpose. Word got to the king that Shadrach, Meshach and Abednego were refusing to bow down and worship the idol.

When the king questioned the Hebrew boys, their response was: "O Nebuchadnezzar, we do not need to defend ourselves before you. If we are thrown into the blazing furnace, the God whom we serve is able to save us. He will rescue us from your power, Your Majesty. But even if he doesn't, we want to make it clear to you, Your Majesty, that we will never serve your gods or worship the gold statue you have set up" (Daniel 3:16-18, NLT).

Those boys had every reason to doubt that day. They had been exiled to a foreign land, had to adjust to a new life away from all their family and traditions… and now they were facing seemingly certain death for their stance. They could have easily just backed down and saved their own life - but they chose instead to trust the God they knew. Even though they did not know what the outcome would be, they still chose to trust and depend on God.

Of course, you know the rest of the story: the king was so enraged that he ordered the furnace to be heated seven times hotter than normal in order to throw the boys into the furnace as punishment for disobeying the king's orders. The guards died throwing Shadrach, Meshach and Abednego in the furnace, but the Hebrew boys did not! And when the king looked into the furnace, he saw a fourth man walking with the Hebrew boys that looked like the Son of God!

In this case of trusting God in spite of what they were faced with, not only were the three Hebrew boys saved miraculously, but the king also sent out another decree to the people of Babylon praising their God.

We can find two more examples of people who had to depend on the Word from the Lord more than they depended on what they felt in Mary and Joseph. That's right! Jesus' earthly parents!

Mary was given a word from the Lord, and despite the fact that she was young, probably scared, and likely didn't feel worthy of the assignment the Lord had for her, she had to choose to depend on what the Lord had told her. She knew what she would be facing in the society of that time: shame of being pregnant without a husband, and possibly fearing for her life since laws at that time permitted the stoning of a woman caught pregnant with a child who was not her husband's. I wonder how many times she had to remind herself of what the angel of the Lord had told her, "Do not be afraid, Mary, for you have found favor with God…" (See Luke 1:26-38).

Of course, Joseph would have been well within his rights for that time and culture to have had Mary put to death, since she was technically carrying a child that was not his… but instead, Joseph decided to break off their relationship privately since he was a kind man. However, the Lord intervened there as well!

According to Matthew 1:20-21, NLT, "As he considered this, an angel of the Lord appeared to him in a dream. "Joseph, son of David," the angel said, "do not be afraid to take Mary as your wife. For the child within her was conceived by the Holy Spirit. And she will have a son, and you are to name him Jesus, for he will save his people from their sins."

Joseph would have had to make the intentional decision to put aside what society would tell him to do in this situation, and to embrace something so foreign to him (and other men of that time) as to welcome a woman who was having a child that was not his.

Don't you think there would be times for both Joseph *and* Mary that they would have doubts and questions? Maybe they wondered if they *really* heard the messenger from the Lord right. Or maybe they were afraid that they were going to mess things up even though the Lord told them what to do.

We don't know from the text if they had perfect faith from that point on, or if, like me, they would have had doubts. What we do know is that Mary and Joseph took the steps necessary to act in faith, whether they felt it or not. They depended more on the word from the Lord than they did their own feelings and insecurities.

I am so glad that even though you have been questioning, doubting and maybe sometimes going through the motions in your own strength, you are here, reading this book with the rest of us with imperfect faith.

And HERE is where you DECIDE SOMETHING.

HERE is where doubt dies and faith grows— because YOU DECIDE TO HAVE FAITH, and God honors that commitment. You DECIDE that no matter what the world looks like, no matter what your bank account looks like, no matter what your kids have done or what your spouse hasn't done, you DECIDE to STILL HAVE FAITH. We decide to look at what's in front of us and not be distracted by the sideshows.

HERE we are drawing our line in the sand, saying, "Devil, you can throw all the doubt you want at me, but at the end of the day, I HAVE DECIDED in whom I will place my trust and confidence!" HERE we DECIDE to trust.

Pray with me: *Lord, thank You. Thank You for not leaving us even when we doubted. Thank You for knowing us well enough to know when, why and how we would doubt You. And thank You for still loving us anyway. God, we give You our doubts, our insecurities and our anxieties. Even though we don't know how things are going to turn out, God, we TRUST You. We have CONFIDENCE that You will keep Your Word, and we make the decision right here, right now, to place our faith in You and only You, Lord! We believe in You and*

Your power, Lord. We have faith in You today. We will have faith in You tomorrow. Thank You, Lord.

Scripture Resources

Then he said to Thomas, 'Put your finger here, and look at my hands. Put your hand into the wound in my side. Don't be faithless any longer. Believe!'"

- **John 20:27, NLT**

Remember, Jesus did not chide or antagonize Thomas for doubting. Rather, He patiently allowed Thomas to find out for himself that Jesus had risen. He wants you to find out for yourself, too!

***

And we are confident that he hears us whenever we ask for anything that pleases him.

- **1 John 5:14, NLT**

He hears us. Would having more faith or trust please Him? Of course! But He hears your prayers too!

***

Yet I still belong to you; you hold my right hand. You guide me with your counsel, leading me to a glorious destiny.

- **Psalm 73:23-24, NLT**

No matter what we have done or haven't done, He doesn't leave us, and we are still His. He cares enough that He will lead us through the doubt into eternity with Him!

***

'Why are you frightened?' he asked. 'Why are your hearts filled with doubt? Look at my hands. Look at my feet. You can see that it's really me. Touch me and make sure that I am not a ghost, because ghosts don't have bodies, as you see that I do.' As he spoke, he showed them his hands and his feet.

- **Luke 24:38-40, NLT**

Even Jesus' disciples had to deal with doubt. Doubt is a normal part of a life of faith. Just as He cared enough to help them overcome their doubt, He will lead us the same way! The key is to make the decision to believe.

***

Don't be afraid, for I am with you. Don't be discouraged, for I am your God. I will strengthen you and help you. I will hold you up with my victorious right hand.

- **Isaiah 41:10, NLT**

He promised that He will be with YOU. PERIOD. It's easy to feel discouraged because we aren't perfect, but He also promises to help us and hold us up. He is our God!

***

But he said to me, 'My grace is sufficient for you, for my power is made perfect in weakness.' Therefore I will boast all the more gladly of my weaknesses, so that the power of Christ may rest upon me.

- **2 Corinthians 12:9, ESV**

Just as He did for Paul, He has grace for you. And He has all the grace you need - for today, tomorrow… He will never run out of grace for you. When we (and our faith) are weak - His power is even more perfect for us!

***

You will keep in perfect peace all who trust in you, all whose thoughts are fixed on you!

- **Isaiah 26:3, NLT**

For me, it's the trust in knowing that if I keep my thoughts on the Lord, He will be my source of peace, even when it seems like everything around me is in chaos.

***

'For I know the plans I have for you,' says the LORD. *'They are plans for good and not for disaster, to give you a future and a hope.'*

- **Jeremiah 29:11, NLT**

That verse has always given me such PEACE, to know that even though I didn't know what was around the corner, HE DID, and He had plans for it. Just because we can't see past the shadows of doubt doesn't mean that He doesn't. He sees much further than we do, and He has plans for us beyond the shadows!

***

And lastly:

The LORD is my shepherd; I shall not want. He makes me lie down in green pastures.
He leads me beside still waters.

He restores my soul.
He leads me in paths of righteousness for his name's sake.

Even though I walk through the valley of the shadow of death, I will fear no evil, for you are with me;

***your rod and your staff,
they comfort me.***

You prepare a table before me in the presence of my enemies;
you anoint my head with oil; my cup overflows.

Surely goodness and mercy shall follow me all the days of my life,
and I shall dwell in the house of the LORD
Forever.

- **Psalm 23:1-6, ESV**

[Emphasis added by author]

About the Author

(Pictured: Tabatha and her son, Col)

Tabatha Rewis was raised in church by her sweet little Baptist grandmother. However, at the age of 15, she saw God work a miracle in her parents' relationship when they reunited and started attending a different church together as a family. It was at that church that she felt the call of God for more hands-on service in the Kingdom, and where she met her husband, Jerry. After she and Jerry married, they moved to Columbus, OH to attend Bible College, where they worked and volunteered for more than five years before entering into full-time ministry as youth and music pastors in Savannah, GA.

Tabatha now serves alongside her husband, Pastor Jerry Rewis, at The Bridge Church of God in

Ochlocknee, GA, where they have been lead pastors for more than ten years now. They have one 20-year-old son (who loves it when Mama calls him her miracle baby, even though he has moved out on his own), and are the primary caregivers for Jerry's mother who lives with them. In addition, Tabatha also works full-time outside the home as an office manager for a busy physical therapy clinic, and considers her job as part of her ministry as well - especially encouraging patients along their recovery journey.

Tabatha's passion for ministry lies in helping women find the truth of their worth, and teaching practical ways for busy moms and women to protect their peace while still reaching out to a chaotic world. Over the last few years, she has developed a passion for studying the Word of God and has three study journals available on Amazon.

Follow Tabatha Rewis @tabrewis

Linktree✱/tabrewis

Subscribe to Tabatha's Podcast: Everyday Imperfect

(Available on all Podcasting Platforms)

Made in United States
Orlando, FL
28 October 2024